# HOW TO

# BALANCE WORK

# AND

# WRITING A BOOK

## Ty A. Patterson

# Introduction

I always knew I wanted to be a writer. I started to make my own books as early as in elementary school. Often getting into trouble for having books under my covers, I quickly became bored with the books I had read over and over at home and said to myself, "I can do this."

At school, I would tear out pieces of my notebook paper, turn them to the landscape position, fold them in half, and add staples down the crease so that it would resemble a real book. I created characters, storylines and my own illustrations.

During the boring classes, I would pull out a little book I made and it would go from hand to hand. Sometimes my little classmates would tap my shoulder and ask, "You got any books today?" That was such a great feeling. Even if I didn't have one, I could make one right then and there. In high school, writing papers and doing presentations was a breeze. I graduated high school with the highest grades in Literature. One of my classmates, Matt Simmons, asked me, "How did you get a grade average of 105?" But hey, I had it, and I ended up being voted *Most Likely to Succeed*. Yes, those were the good old days.

After some years of not-so-academic college years, I realized that I had pushed my love for writing right up under those covers from my childhood.

Two children later, it never seemed to be the right time to start writing. I was either working or just too busy. However, nothing made me happy until I just remembered those word I said years ago, "I can do this."

Whether you are working full-time or part-time, there is no

better time than the present. Here are the tips that helped me on my long lost journey to becoming an author. Today, I write books, poetry, songs, and scripts.

I followed my dream of writing and so can you!

1. Be aware of your work environment.

Make sure that writing will not conflict with your job tasks. If you work in a fast paced environment, or high volume call center, wait until you are home or can get to a coffee shop, bookstore, or library.

Make sure that working on your book is not illegal. Do not break company policy to write because everyone is not always willing to bend the rules for you.

2. Keep your supplies near you in an unmarked carrier at all times.

Your bag of supplies should not bring attention to anything you are doing that is outside of work tasks. Black, brown or gray bags are a good choice.

If you are not prepared to write, you may have great thoughts that you cannot capture, which is why you should never leave your supplies at home. Driving, in the shower, after a dream, or during a conversation are some moments when you have profound thoughts and need to write them down quickly. Otherwise, you may forget what you wanted to write, especially if you have a busy schedule.

Supplies may include, but are not limited to: cell phone, a jump drive, paper clips, pens, pencils, mini stapler, folders, laptop, notebook, post- its, highlighters, white out, other helpful books, shoulder bag, dictionary (if there is no access to Microsoft office).

3. Be willing to sacrifice sleep, lunches or breaks to write

You cannot predict when a thought will come to you and you need to be ready. If your place of employment does not permit sending emails, use of cell phones or internet on the computer, you would not be able to simply send the thoughts to yourself. Therefore, it would be best to keep a journal. Many times a thought comes to us and we think that just because it is a great thought, surely we will remember. Then as soon as your break is over and you try to find a pen and paper, your thoughts aren't as vivid. Of course, the fastest way to records your thoughts is to put it in your phone if you can.

# 4. Pick and choose your battles

Every day may not be the best day to write. If you are having a bad or crazy day, you may find it hard to focus if you are writing a positive book. On the contrary, it may be the perfect time if you are writing drama or horror.

In your free time, do not write if you simply cannot focus. Use that time to meditate, pray or read something positive so that your day does not end on a bad note. Do not end your day arguing or watching anything negative. This may mean turning off the news or staying off of social media. Instead, watch a great movie, visit your favorite store, or eat some yummy ice cream. Take your mind away from writing, and try again tomorrow.

# 5. Conduct surveys.

Find people that you trust and let them hear concepts and give you their opinions and suggestions. (Book titles, chapter names, and even subject matter). But be careful giving away too much information or taking too much advice.

See how quickly you can draw a reader in with the things that you write.

Ask if they would buy a book like that, or if they know someone who would.

You can also do your own surveys by comparing articles that you find online about catchy titles, the best way to publish, costs, or what to expect after completing your book.

# 6. Network.

You don't know who knows who these days. Find out who your connections are with authors, poets, artists, bloggers, magazines and media, or who is simply a book junkie! There a freelance editors who may be willing to help and there are readers on YouTube that give book reviews. Reach out to people with the most followers and see if they can assist you.

Do not be afraid of Social Media, but be very professional with it even if you need to adjust the one(s) you have. Limit what you post because your co-workers can find you and if you post that you have been writing, it may seem as if you are neglecting your job tasks even if it is not illegal.

For example, posting, "I enjoyed working on my novel at work today", may get you in trouble with your boss.

This goes back to #1.

# 7. Believe in yourself.

I hope that these tips help you along the way of becoming that great writer that you have dreamt about.

Do not worry about writer's block or any other set-backs that may come your way. Life happens, but always tell yourself, "I Can Do This".